FUN and GAMES
Everyday Play

WRITTEN BY **Celeste Cortright**

ILLUSTRATED BY **Sophie Fatus**

Barefoot Books
Step inside a story

It's time to play! Let's laugh and learn.
Join in the fun and take a turn.

In **hide-and-seek**, the counting down
will send us running all around.

We find a clever hiding spot.
Here they come, ready or not!

Let's have some fun with **dominoes!**
We'll place them carefully in rows.

We try to find a matching tile,

Or else we draw one from the pile.

Hoop rolling is a timeless game.
To keep them upright is our aim!

We guide the rim with hooks or sticks,
And sometimes try out fancy tricks.

A **dollhouse** is a special toy
That everybody can enjoy.

We role-play while we all explore,

With action figures, dolls and more.

Let's take turns playing **spinning tops**.
We twirl the stem and then we watch!

The fast rotation helps them go
And keeps them balanced 'til they slow.

With **tangrams**, we will try to make
An image out of seven shapes.

The puzzle's picture keeps evolving,
'Til we're finished problem-solving!

When we **jump rope** we skip our feet,
Then swing the rope and keep the beat.

We make small circles with our wrists,
And focus hard so no one trips!

Our **cuddly toys** are cherished friends
Who join us while we play pretend.

Throughout a day of highs and lows,
We have someone to snuggle close.

We can be quiet or make noise
With lots of different games and toys.

We sometimes lose and sometimes win,
But most of all — we *all* join in!

Hide-and-Seek

Hide-and-seek has been played for as long as there have been children. It is known by many names around the world. It can be played indoors or outdoors, with two or more players. Igbo children in Nigeria play a game called Oro, which combines hide-and-seek and the thrilling chase of a game of tag!

Dominoes

The first form of dominoes came from China 1,000 years ago. There are many different games you can play with these small tiles, by yourself or with friends. Many games focus on matching up the numbers, but you can also just have fun lining the tiles up and knocking them over. Dominoes are very popular in Jamaica, where players finish their game by slamming the final piece on the table!

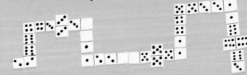

Hoop Rolling

Hoops can be made of metal, vines, wood, bamboo and many other materials. In ancient Egypt, hoops were pushed around using plants called reeds. There are many different ways to play this game, either using a stick or your hand to roll the hoop along as you run to keep up.

Dollhouses

People have been creating dolls for thousands of years, but the very first dollhouse (or doll's house) was made over 600 years ago in Germany. Dollhouses were originally created for adults to show off their collections of miniatures. Perhaps the most famous dollhouse belonged to Queen Mary of England. It had running water, electricity and little working cars!

Spinning Tops

Some of the oldest spinning tops, possibly over 5,000 years old, were made of clay and found in Iraq. They can also be made from natural materials such as fruit, nuts and seeds. Spinning tops have been discovered on every continent except Antarctica. A carved spinning top was even found in Egyptian King Tut's tomb!

Tangrams

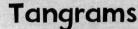

Tangrams are seven flat shapes that, when put together, create a perfect square. Believed to have originally come from China, this puzzle game uses geometry, or the positioning of shapes, to solve mathematical problems. Using all seven pieces in a tangram set, there are hundreds of pictures you can create!

Jump Ropes

The first jump ropes were made of vines and other natural materials. They have been used in many cultures for a very long time. Also known as skipping ropes, they are popular all around the world both for fun and for exercise. Skipping can be done on your own or with friends. A Japanese rope skipper once jumped over 150,000 times in 24 hours!

Cuddly Toys

From our earliest days, cuddly toys give us comfort as we grow. The very first cuddly toys were made from bits of fabric then filled with straw. Known as rag dolls, they were created by the Romans thousands of years ago. The original teddy bear was named after American President Theodore "Teddy" Roosevelt.

Since childhood, **Celeste Cortright** has loved being silly, solving puzzles and playing competitive games. She currently lives in the city of Boston, Massachusetts, USA with her partner and cat, where she works as a design director and still enjoys playing pretend. Celeste has also written *The More We Get Together* and *Ready, Set, Go!* for Barefoot Books.

Sophie Fatus was born in Paris into a family of artists and now lives in Florence with her partner and two cats. She is a full-time illustrator whose artwork is always filled with fun. In her spare time, she loves to create silly sculptures such as horses, birds or cat-shaped chairs. Sophie has illustrated many projects for Barefoot Books, most recently *Global Kids*.